Success in English
Reading

Barry Scholes
Anita Scholes
Stuart Bell
Series Editor: Jayne de Courcy

Ages 9–11

BOOK **3**

Contents

Collins Educational
An Imprint of HarperCollinsPublishers

The ⭐3⭐ Steps to Success ...

Step 1

Key skills practice

⭐ *Success in English Book 3* provides practice in a number of important English reading skills. These skills are the ones that your child needs to master in order to achieve a high level in the English National Test at the end of Key Stage 2. This book builds on the reading skills practised in *Success in English Book 1*.

⭐ Each chapter takes one reading skill and works through it in straightforward steps. At the end of each chapter there is a *Test yourself* section containing questions to answer. This allows you and your child to see how well they have understood the skill taught.

⭐ This in-depth teaching and practice ensures that your child will achieve real understanding of each skill.

Step 2

Practice with National Test questions

⭐ At the end of the book there is a Reading Test paper which is similar to the one that your child will have to sit in his/her KS2 English National Test.

⭐ This Test-style paper allows you to see the sort of passages and questions your child will meet in the Reading Test. The questions require your child to demonstrate all the reading skills taught in the book.

⭐ Your child can do this Test paper immediately after working on the skills chapters. You might, however, prefer to wait and ask him/her to do it a little later to check that he/she really does have a solid grasp of the reading skills needed.

Step 3

Improving your child's performance

⭐ The book contains detailed *Answers and Guidance* to both the *Test yourself* sections and the Reading Test paper.

⭐ The authors, one of whom is a KS2 Test Examiner, provide model answers and also explain what the questions are trying to assess. They show what sort of answers will score high marks in the Reading Test and why.

⭐ In this way, you can work with your child to help him/her improve his/her performance in the KS2 English National Test.

Help with timing

★ As the English National Test is timed, it is important that your child learns to answer questions within a time limit.

★ Each *Test yourself* section and the Test paper give target times for answering the questions. If you choose to, you can ask your child to time himself/herself when answering the questions. You can then compare his/her time against the target times provided in the Answers and Guidance. In this way, you will form a good idea of whether your child is working at the right rate to complete the National Test Reading paper successfully.

Progression

★ *Success in English* is aimed at 9–11 year-olds who are in Years 5 and 6 of primary school. There is in-built progression in the series: each book builds on skills taught in previous books.

★ To get the most out of *Success in English*, it is important that your child works through all four books in sequence. If you are buying this series for your child who is aged 9/10 (Year 5), then buy Books 1 and 2, and Books 3 and 4 at age 10/11 (Year 6). If your child is already in Year 6, then it is still advisable to work through from Book 1 to Book 4, to ensure that your child benefits from the progression built into the series.

Note to teachers

★ This book, and the other four titles in the *Success in English* series, are designed for use at home and in schools in Years 5 and 6. They focus on the key reading and writing skills that will raise children's performance in the English National Test.

★ You can use the books in class or give them to children for homework to ensure that they are fully prepared for their English National Test.

1 Reading information texts for clues

What's it all about?

★ In this chapter you will learn how to find clues in an information text.

★ You will be learning how to use such clues to answer questions about things the writer does not tell you directly.

★ Your National Test Reading paper will include questions that expect you to use clues to work out the answers.

How to read an information text for clues

This is part of an autobiography called *Coming to England* by Floella Benjamin. As a young girl she leaves her home in Trinidad, Jamaica, to live in England. When she goes to her first English school she finds many things are strange, but one of them is particularly unpleasant.

The Cruel Game

There wasn't a stall selling treats in the playground but the children did play clapping and skipping games which made me feel at home. There was one game, however, which I didn't understand at first but in no time at all I began to hate. The first time I saw the children play it, I knew it was wrong and cruel. I was standing next to the wall with the painted bull's-eye when some boys came up and spat strange words at me, words that I had never heard before but from their faces I knew they were not nice. They were words which told me that I was different from them and that they felt my kind shouldn't be in their country. I looked at them, confused and baffled like a trapped, helpless creature. What was 'my kind' and why shouldn't I be in the country I was brought up to love? The land of hope and glory, mother of the free. I began to feel angry and violent as I stood and watched their ugly faces jeering at me.

But they might as well be talking in a foreign language because I didn't understand the words they were shouting. I didn't let them make me cry though; I had learnt how to be tough during the time Marmie had left us in Trinidad. When I got home and asked Marmie what the words meant, she looked sad and sat us all down and slowly explained that because of the colour of our skin some people were going to be cruel and nasty to us. But we must be strong, make something of ourselves and never let them get the better of us. That was the day I realised that in the eyes of some people in this world I was not a person but a colour.

I looked down at my hands and desperately tried to understand why my colour meant so much to some and disturbed them so deeply. In Trinidad there were people of different races, from all over the world and they lived together in harmony. No one felt threatened or was made to feel bad because of his or her colour. So why all the fuss in England? I felt so confused.

Let's see if you can answer this question:

How is this autobiographical account similar to a story?

Like a story, this autobiographical account has a setting and characters, and tells about events. A good answer is:

This account is similar to a story because it has a setting, the school playground, and a main character, Floella Benjamin, who is also the narrator. It tells about the cruel game the other children play on Floella and what happens when she tells Marmie. Like most stories, it is written in the past tense.

Now let's see if you can answer this question:

> **In what ways is the playground in England similar to, and different from, the one the writer knew in Trinidad?**

We are not told directly what a school playground in Trinidad is like, but there are clues in the sentence: 'There wasn't a stall selling treats in the playground but the children did play clapping and skipping games which made me feel at home.' From this we know that in Trinidad, unlike in England, school playgrounds have stalls selling treats. We can also tell that children there play clapping and skipping games, because it was the playing of those games in the English school that made the writer feel at home.

A good answer is:

Playgrounds in England do not have stalls selling treats like in Trinidad, but children play clapping and skipping games in both places.

Test yourself

Answer these questions by using clues in the passage.

1 Why do you think the writer did not understand the words the children shouted in their cruel game?

2 Explain why the writer felt confused by the game.

3 Why do you think the writer did not tell her teacher about it?

4 The text says 'Marmie looked sad and sat us all down'. Who do you think Marmie is, and who does the writer mean by 'all'?

5 What do you think the writer means by 'to some people in this world I was not a person but a colour'?

Answers and Guidance are given on p.31. *How long did you take?*

2 Using evidence from information texts

What's it all about?

★ In this chapter you will learn how to answer questions using evidence in the text.

★ Your answers will sometimes need to explain things in your own words, using the evidence you have found in the text. They will sometimes need to include direct quotations (words and phrases which you lift from the text and put quotation marks around).

★ Your National Test Reading paper will include questions that expect you to support your answers with evidence.

How to use evidence from the text

Read this passage.

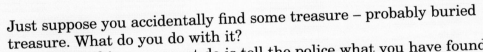

Finding treasure

Just suppose you accidentally find some treasure – probably buried treasure. What do you do with it?

The first thing you must do is tell the police what you have found, or take it to them. It is not yours to keep – not yet. It might belong to somebody, or it might even be Treasure Trove. Treasure Trove is anything made of gold or silver that is found in the ground or in some secret place, and the owner of which can not be found. In Scotland, anything ancient that you find, whether it's made of gold or silver or other material, is always Treasure Trove.

After you have told the police about the treasure, they then tell the Coroner. This is a person who holds an enquiry, called an inquest, when somebody dies unexpectedly. The Coroner will then hold an inquest on what you've found, just as if it's a dead body! If the Coroner decides that the treasure you have found really is Treasure Trove, then it belongs to the Queen. (If you find treasure in some parts of Cornwall, then it belongs to the Duke of Cornwall instead.) That means that you can't keep whatever you have found, but you will still be paid the full amount of what it is worth. An example of this happening was when somebody was on holiday in Torquay, in Devon, when they saw a bit of shiny metal sticking up out of the sand on the beach. When it was pulled out, it was discovered to be a gold circlet dating from the time of the Saxons. It was Treasure Trove, and the person who found it was given £5,000, which was what the treasure was worth at the time.

If, on the other hand, the Coroner decides that the treasure you have found is not Treasure Trove, then you can keep it. Or, if you like, you can send it to the British Museum and they'll either buy it from you or sell it and then give you the money, so you don't lose out either way.

There is one important thing to remember. You must report what you have found *straight away*. If you don't, and the police find out later, then you'll most likely get nothing at all and the treasure will be taken from you – and serve you right!

Let's see if you can answer this question:

> **What is wrong with this statement? 'In Scotland anything you find is always Treasure Trove.'**

Scan the text for the key words 'Treasure Trove'. When you have found them read that part of the text carefully for information about Treasure Trove in Scotland. We are told: 'In Scotland, anything <u>ancient</u> that you find, whether it's made of gold or silver or other material, is always Treasure Trove.' The important word for us here is 'ancient'. If you find something in Scotland which is *not* ancient then it is *not* Treasure Trove.

You can use this evidence in your answer. Notice that part of the answer is in your own words and part is quoted from the passage. Use quotation marks where necessary:

In Scotland something you find is only Treasure Trove if it is ancient. We know this because the text says Treasure Trove is "anything ancient that you find".

Now let's see if you can answer this question:

> Explain what you must do if you find a number of ancient silver coins buried in the ground.

This question asks you to *explain*. So just using words from the passage will not give a full enough answer, nor show that you have understood what you have read. You need to find the evidence, and then write it out in your own words as an explanation.

The evidence for our explanation is in two places in the passage. At the beginning of paragraph two we are told: 'The first thing you must do is tell the police what you have found, or take it to them.' The second sentence in paragraph five tells us: 'You must report what you have found *straight away*.' Put the two pieces of evidence together for a full answer:

> If you find ancient silver coins buried in the ground you must report the find to the police straight away.

Test yourself

Answer these questions by using evidence from the passage.

1 Say if each of these is Treasure Trove.
Give a reason for each answer.
  a an ancient silver coin you find in a garden
  b a gold chain lost many years ago by someone you know
  c a bronze age brooch found in England
  d a bronze age brooch found in Scotland

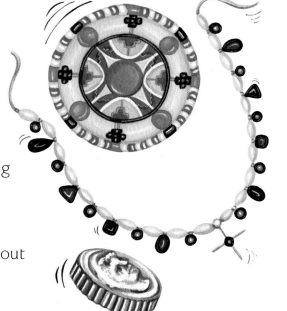

2 What happens if the Coroner decides something you find really is Treasure Trove?

3 If it is not Treasure Trove what happens then?

4 Which words tell you what the writer thinks about people who wait some time before reporting what they have found?

Answers and Guidance are given on p.31. *How long did you take?*

How to use clues and evidence

Read this passage carefully.

The Girl at the Well

All right then, if it's a story you're wanting, throw another log on the fire. The winters strike colder now than they used to do when I was a young man in Britain: and I'll tell you ...

Eburacum was a frontier station in my father's day; your great-grandfather's. But Roman rule spread northward in one way and another; and by the time I was posted up there as Eagle Bearer to the Ninth Legion it wasn't a frontier station any more, and the settlement that had gathered itself together under the fortress walls had become a sizeable town, with a forum where the business of the place was carried on, and wine shops, and temples to half a score of different gods.

Well, so I was ambling up the narrow, crooked street behind the temple of Sulis on one of those dark edge-of-spring evenings when it seems as though all the colour has drained out of the world and left only the grey behind. I was off duty and I was bored. I'd been down at the lower end of the town to look at some new young fighting cocks that Kaeso had for sale, but I hadn't liked the look of any that he had shown me, and taking it all in all, I was feeling thoroughly out at elbows with the world. And then I rounded the corner of the temple garden; and there, at the well that bubbled up from under the wall, a few paces further up the street, a girl was drawing water. And I knew I'd been wrong about there being no colour left in the world, because her hair lit up that grey street like a dandelion growing on a stubble pile. – No, that's not right either, it was redder and more sparkling; a colour that you could warm your hands at. And the braids of it, hanging forward over her shoulders 'thick as a swordsman's wrist' as the saying goes.

You can guess the next bit, I dare say.

Let's see if you can answer this question:

> **Which words tell you that the storyteller is talking to a younger person?**

We need to look for evidence in the text which proves this. The evidence is in the first line of the second paragraph: 'Eburacum was a frontier station <u>in my father's day; your great-grandfather's</u>.' This means that the storyteller's father lived at the same time as the listener's great-grandfather, proving that the storyteller is talking to a younger person.

A good answer uses this evidence by quoting words from the text:

> The words "my father's day; your great-grandfather's" tell us he is speaking to a younger person.

Now let's see if you can answer this question:

> **Who do you think Sulis was? What makes you think this?**

First scan the passage for the name 'Sulis'. You will read 'Well, so I was ambling up the narrow, crooked street behind the temple of Sulis...'. In the previous sentence we read that in the forum there were 'temples to half a score of different gods'. These two facts mean Sulis was a god.

A good answer is:

> Sulis was a god, because the passage refers to the temple of Sulis.

Test yourself

Answer these questions by using clues and evidence from the passage.

1 What evidence is there to show that Eburacum had become a sizeable town?

2 Who do you think Kaeso was? Say why you think this.

3 What do you think 'out at elbows with the world' means? What makes you think so?

4 Which words show the sudden effect the girl had on the storyteller?

5 Write three details that show the story is set in Roman Britain.

6 Explain, giving your reasons, what you think will happen next?

Answers and Guidance are given on p.32. *How long did you take?*

11

What's it all about?	★	In this chapter you will learn how to develop your understanding of characters – what they feel, what they are thinking and why they behave as they do.
	★	In most stories, the writer will tell you some information about the characters but will leave you to 'read for clues' in order to find out more.
	★	Your National Test Reading paper will include questions which test how well you understand the characters in a story from what they do, think, say and feel.

How to answer questions about character

Read this extract.

The School Teacher

I was born in this mountain village longer ago than I like to remember. I was to have been a shepherd like my grandfather and his grandfather before him, but when I was three, an accident left me with a limp. Shepherding wasn't ever going to be possible, so I became a teacher instead.

For nearly forty years now, I have been the schoolmaster here. I live alone in a house by the school, content with my own company and my music. To play my hunting horn high in the mountains, and to hear its echo soaring with the eagles, is as close as I have been to complete happiness.

Yet I suppose you could say that I became a sort of shepherd after all: I shepherd children instead of sheep, that's all. I teach them, and I'm a kind of uncle to them even after they've left school. They think I'm a bit eccentric – I play my horn and I talk to myself more than I should. Like all children, they can be a bit cruel from time to time. They call me 'Three Legs' or 'Long John Silver' when they think I'm not listening, but you have to put up with that.

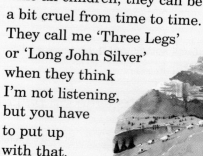

We are people whose lives are ruled by sheep, by the seasons, and above all by the mountains. We make cheese here, sheep's cheese. You won't find a better cheese anywhere, that's a promise. Almost all the families have a flock of sheep which they graze in the fields around the village, but when the snows clear, they take them up on to the mountain pastures for the sweet summer grass. The cows go too, and the horses and pigs.

Snow cuts us off for at least three months of every winter, sometimes more, and then we are left to ourselves. But it's a peaceful place at any time of year. The winding road from the valley ends in the village square. Beyond us are the mountains, and beyond the mountains, the sky. We are a world of our own and we like it that way. We are used to it. The life is hard but predictable. People are born, people die. We have our blizzards and our droughts, no one ever has enough money and the roof always needs repairing.

Let's see if you can answer this question:

> How does the narrator feel about living alone? How can you tell?

The second paragraph tells us: 'I live alone in a house by the school, content with my own company and my music.' This gives you the evidence needed for your answer:

The narrator does not mind living alone. We know this because it says he is content with his own company and music.

Now let's see if you can answer this question:

> **What does he enjoy most? Which words tell you this?**

The evidence we need for our answer is in the words: 'To play my hunting horn high in the mountains, and to hear its echo soaring with the eagles, is as close as I have been to complete happiness.' A good answer will quote those words:

> What he enjoys most is playing his hunting horn high in the mountains. The words which tell us are "To play my hunting horn high in the mountains, and to hear its echo soaring with the eagles, is as close as I have been to complete happiness."

Test yourself

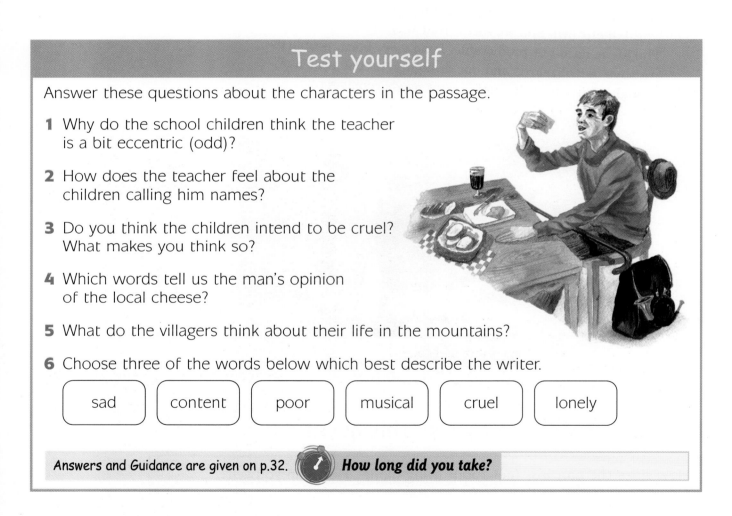

Answer these questions about the characters in the passage.

1 Why do the school children think the teacher is a bit eccentric (odd)?

2 How does the teacher feel about the children calling him names?

3 Do you think the children intend to be cruel? What makes you think so?

4 Which words tell us the man's opinion of the local cheese?

5 What do the villagers think about their life in the mountains?

6 Choose three of the words below which best describe the writer.

| sad | content | poor | musical | cruel | lonely |

Answers and Guidance are given on p.32.   *How long did you take?*

What's it all about?

★ In this chapter you will learn how to read texts in order to find out what the writer's own opinion is on the subject he or she is writing about.

★ An opinion is what someone thinks or believes about something. Sometimes writers make their own views very clear. Sometimes you have to read the text very carefully for clues about what their opinion is.

★ Your National Test Reading paper may include a question which tests whether you can find out, and explain, what the writer's opinion is about the subject he or she is writing about.

How to find out the writer's opinion

Newspapers contain a mix of fact and opinion. A fact is something which is true. An opinion is what someone thinks or believes. It may or may not be true. As you read these cuttings try to sort the opinions from the facts.

Dear Editor,

Five weeks ago I wrote to a local councillor about the streetlights that had failed in my part of Capshaw.

One of these lights is meant to light a stretch of canal towpath, but which is now in complete darkness at night. This is a very dangerous spot and it is only a matter of time before someone has an accident.

Yesterday I received a letter from the lighting department at Capshaw Council informing me that although this particular light needed only a replacement bulb, to fit one would require special hydraulic equipment, and because of this the lamp is unlikely to be repaired for some time.

I'm sure all ratepayers will find this response quite unacceptable. Do we have to wait for a serious accident before Capshaw Council is prepared to attend to urgent needs?

Yours
Disgusted ratepayer

Let's see if you can answer this question:

> What does the writer of the letter think might happen soon in his or her part of Capshaw? Why does the writer think so?

The writer's opinion is: 'This is a very dangerous spot and it is only a matter of time before someone has an accident.' The facts which support this opinion can be found in the first two paragraphs: streetlights have failed in a part of Capshaw, and one light is intended to light a canal towpath. A good answer would be:

> The writer thinks that eventually there will be an accident at the part of the canal towpath where a streetlight has failed.

Now let's see if you can answer this question:

> What does the writer think about the letter he or she received from Capshaw Council?

In their letter Capshaw Council claim that to fit a replacement bulb would take some time because special hydraulic equipment is needed. The writer's opinion is that is 'all ratepayers will find this response quite unacceptable'. A good answer will make clear what the writer finds unacceptable:

> The writer thinks that the delay in replacing the bulb is unacceptable, and he believes all ratepayers will agree with him.

Capshaw Chronicle

United beat Darnley in exciting opener

Capshaw United started the new season in fine style by beating Darnley City 2-0.

To a man, United showed tremendous determination from the kick-off. At first the pressure came from City, but United's tight defence proved hard to penetrate. On the few occasions they broke through they found keeper Phil Owens on top form, producing three breathtaking saves.

The second half began with an exciting goal from United's Sam Peters, and within a few minutes Ben Holden drove a ball past City's Lee Salter into the corner of the net.

The game came to a nailbiting finish as City repeatedly attacked United's goal, but fortunately the home side's defence remained intact through to the final whistle.

Phil Owens was on top form

Accident blackspot remains

It may be that Highstones Road has been made safer after repairs to the road surface and the installation of kerb stones on the sharp bend.

But Councillor Bill Evans said today, "Highstones Road will remain an accident blackspot until Capshaw Council sees sense and reduces the unsafe 60mph speed limit."

Three pedestrians and two car drivers have been killed there in the past two years.

Bus pass charge scrapped

Capshaw Council have been persuaded by public pressure to scrap its £10 charge for pensioners' bus passes.

Councillor Geoffrey Dobson, who has been campaigning against the charge for over two years, said, "Capshaw was the only Council in the county to impose this cruel charge on pensioners."

CLLR GEOFFREY DOBSON

Highstones Road – accident blackspot

Test yourself

Answer these questions about the writers' opinions in the letter and the three newspaper articles.

1 Which word shows most clearly how strongly the letter writer feels?

2 Find three phrases in the football report which show that the reporter thought United played well.

3 Which team do you think the reporter supported? How can you tell?

4 In the accident blackspot report, what is Councillor Bill Evans' opinion of the improvements to Highstones Road? Which words tell you this?

5 In the same report, what does the reporter think about the improvements? What makes you think so?

6 In the bus pass charges report, which word does the councillor use which shows his opinion of those charges?

Answers and Guidance are given on p.32. *How long did you take?*

What's it all about?

★ In this chapter you will learn how to comment on the words and phrases authors use in their stories.

★ Your National Test Reading paper may include questions which ask you to comment on the author's use of language.

How to comment on an author's use of language

Read this extract from the story of Beowulf.

Grendel

Through the dark night a darker shape slid. A sinister figure shrithed down from the moors, over high shoulders, sopping tussocks, over sheep-runs, over gurgling streams. It shrithed towards the timbered hall, huge and hairy and slightly stooping. Its long arms swung loosely.

One man was snoring, one mumbling, one coughing; all the Geats guarding Heorot had fallen asleep – all except one, one man watching.

For a moment the shape waited outside the hall. It cocked an ear. It began to quiver. Its hair bristled. Then it grasped the great ring-handle and swung open the door, the mouth of Heorot. It lunged out of the darkness and into the circle of dim candlelight, it took a long stride across the patterned floor.

Through half-closed eyes Beowulf was watching, and through barred teeth he breathed one word, 'Grendel'. The name of the monster, the loathsome syllables.

Grendel saw the knot of sleeping warriors and his eyes shone with an unearthly light. He lurched towards the nearest man, a brave Geat called Leofric, scooped him up and, with one ghastly claw, choked the scream in his throat. Then the monster ripped him apart, bit into his body, drank the blood from his veins, devoured huge pieces; within one minute he had swallowed the whole man, even his feet and hands.

Still the Geats slept. The air in Heorot was thick with their sleep, thicker still with death and the stench of the monster.

Grendel slobbered spittle and blood; his first taste of flesh only made him more ravenous. He wheeled round towards Beowulf, stooped, reached out for him, and Beowulf...

Beowulf leaped up and stayed the monster's outstretched arm.

Grendel grunted and pulled back. And at that sound, all the other Geats were instantly awake. They grabbed their swords, they backed off, they shouted for Beowulf.

Let's see if you can answer this question:

> **Find three words from the passage which show that Grendel moved in an unpleasant way.**

The author uses several words which show how the creature moved: 'slid', 'shrithed', 'lunged', 'took a long stride', 'lurched' and 'wheeled'. Of these it is 'slid', 'shrithed', 'lunged' and 'lurched' which suggest something unpleasant. Any three of these would be acceptable as an answer.

We will look at the language poets use in Chapter 9.

Test yourself

Answer these questions about words used in the passage.

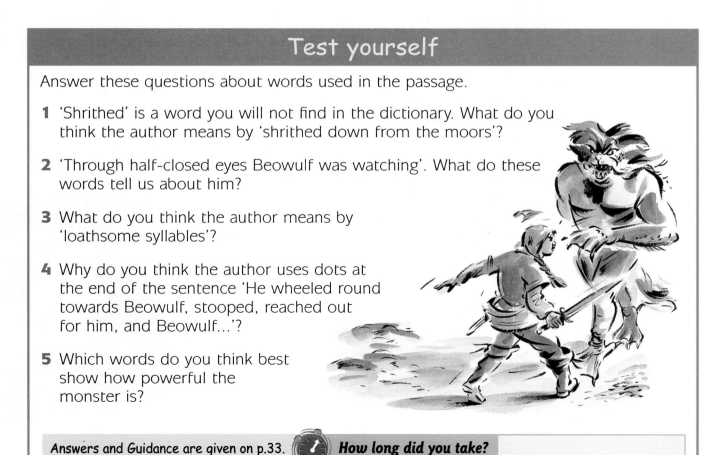

1 'Shrithed' is a word you will not find in the dictionary. What do you think the author means by 'shrithed down from the moors'?

2 'Through half-closed eyes Beowulf was watching'. What do these words tell us about him?

3 What do you think the author means by 'loathsome syllables'?

4 Why do you think the author uses dots at the end of the sentence 'He wheeled round towards Beowulf, stooped, reached out for him, and Beowulf...'?

5 Which words do you think best show how powerful the monster is?

Answers and Guidance are given on p.33.   *How long did you take?*

What's it all about?

★ In this chapter you will learn how to comment on words and phrases used in information texts.

★ Your National Test Reading paper may include questions which ask you to comment on the author's use of language.

'HEIGHT, THE SIZE OF A BIG DOG'
'several sightings'
'Weight 110 lbs'
'two runaway pigs'
'five-month old'
'FAST-FLOWING'

How to comment on the use of language

Read this newspaper report.

The Grunt Escape

Daily Mail Reporter

On the run, pigs who saved themselves from getting the pork chop

THE DESCRIPTION of the two fugitives is as follows.

Height, the size of a big dog. Colour, pink with ginger bristles all over. Weight, 110lbs – but with a deceptive turn of speed.

Oh, yes – and not averse to swimming across fast-flowing rivers, especially when they're keen to save their bacon.

Two runaway pigs were enjoying their fifth day of freedom yesterday after escaping from an abattoir seconds before they were due for the chop.

The five-month-old Ginger Tamworth boars made a break for it on market day at Malmesbury, Wiltshire, last Thursday after a fellow porker was led off to its fate.

The plucky pair ran rings round slaughterhouse men in the abattoir yard before forcing their way through a hole in the fence.

At first it seemed they had made a pig's ear of their great escape because their path was blocked by the River Avon.

But they astonished their pursuers by diving in and swimming five yards to the other side, sticking their snouts in the air to breathe. There have been several sightings since in the back gardens and vegetable patches of Malmesbury.

Let's see if you can answer these questions:

> **Why does the report have the headline 'The Grunt Escape'?**

The reporter is using a pun – a play on words. The word 'grunt' is used to replace 'great' in the expression 'great escape' because pigs grunt and the report is about pigs. This question tests if you understand what a pun is, so make it clear in your answer that you know the headline is playing on words. A good answer is:

The headline is a play on words. It says 'grunt escape' instead of 'great escape' because the report is about pigs.

Now read this article about the rainforest.

Eating the rainforest

Hamburger, cheeseburger, chilliburger, quarter-pounder ... yummy! We love them, and we buy millions from fast food restaurants every year. They're cheap, they're very quick, they taste good, and they don't even do you much harm. But when you chomp into a burger, do you ever stop to think about how that burger has reached you? The simple truth is, your favourite fast food snack could be doing more damage to the planet than just about anything else you come into daily contact with.

Fast food started in America, just over 30 years ago. In those days, most of the meat for the burgers came from cattle farms in Central American countries like Costa Rica. The trouble was, and is, that the land in those countries is not really suitable for beef farming. First, large areas of rainforest have to be chopped down to provide grazing land for cattle. With the trees gone, the soil soon loses its nutrients, and after a few years, it becomes useless for grazing cattle. It's wasted. The forest cannot be replaced and the cattle farmer has to go somewhere else, to begin the destruction again. Since the late 1950s, most of the rainforest in Central America has been lost this way, and a huge area in the Amazon forest in Brazil as well.

The writer of the rainforest article begins in a light-hearted way. Which word does the writer use which particularly shows this?

A good answer is:

The word 'yummy' particularly shows this because it is an informal word you wouldn't expect to see in a serious article.

Test yourself

Answer these questions about words used in the two articles.

1 At what point does the reporter reveal that the fugitives are pigs? Which words tell you?

2 Why does the reporter use expressions such as 'save their bacon', 'due for the chop' and 'made a pig's ear'?

3 Explain the title of the rainforest article.

4 Why do you think the writer uses the word 'chomp' rather than 'eat'?

5 Which words first show us that the article on the rainforest is not really about enjoying hamburgers?

6 Which two words in the second paragraph do you think best sum up the effect of beef farming on the soils of the rainforest?

Answers and Guidance are given on p.33.   **How long did you take?**

What's it all about?

★ In this chapter you will learn how to recognise differences between types of story.

★ You will need to think about what makes one type of story different from another.

★ Your National Test Reading paper may include questions which ask you about story types.

How to recognise differences between story types

There are many different types of story: mystery, adventure, science fiction (sci-fi), myths, legends, fables, fantasy, historical etc. As you read these extracts, ask yourself which types of story they are.

1

A blaze sprang up and Caspian almost screamed with the shock as the sudden light revealed the face that was looking into his own. It was not a man's face that was looking into his own. It was not a man's face but a badger's, though larger and friendlier and more intelligent than the face of any badger he had seen before. And it had certainly been talking. He saw, too, that he was on a bed of heather, in a cave. By the fire sat two little bearded men, so much wilder and shorter and hairier and thicker than Doctor Cornelius that he know them at once for real Dwarfs, ancient Dwarfs with not a drop of human blood in their veins. And Caspian knew that he had found the Old Narnians at last.

2

The tremor woke Marcou instantly. Even the slightest vibration was unusual in a Gundran spaceship. He glanced at the large illuminated dial set in the wall of his cabin. The needle pointed at 257. Too early to get up; he usually rose at 300. As he drifted off to sleep again the visual address unit in the corner of his room suddenly flickered to life and the familiar face of his uncle appeared on the small screen.

'This is a purple alert!' Dabvich Kendron said. 'The Azura has been hit by a small meteorite. The long-range communications system is damaged and we are no longer in contact with Gundra. There is also a fault in the propulsion unit. Everything possible is being done, but in the meantime all crew members must remain on purple alert. Repeat, purple alert.'

"I think that's far enough, Angela," I pleaded. "We'd better stop now."

The cart went on rolling and I could sense that it was gaining speed.

"Please, Angela," I said. "Let's stop." Then I heard a sort of scuffle and a thump, so I opened my eyes to see what she was up to.

Well, I got such a fright I nearly had kittens. Angela wasn't there. I was sitting in that cab all by myself and it was racing away down the hill getting faster and faster and all I could think about was that great big brick wall at the bottom where the road went round the corner.

"Angela!" I shouted. I swivelled round in my seat and just managed to catch a glimpse of her through the pile of crates in the back. There she was, picking herself up off the pavement and brushing the dust off her denim dungarees.

Let's see if you can answer this question:

> **What features of a fantasy story does the first passage have?**

Fantasy stories are often set in strange lands with magical creatures and people. Even everyday animals can often talk and behave like people. This passage has a talking badger and 'real Dwarfs, ancient Dwarfs with not a drop of human blood in their veins'. The setting is a cave, a place where dwarfs are often found in fantasy stories. You could include all these things in your answer:

This passage has a number of features of a fantasy story. It is set in a cave where there are ancient dwarfs and a talking badger.

Now let's see if you can answer this question:

> **What kind of story is the second passage? How can you tell?**

The second passage is science fiction (sci-fi). Such stories usually take place in future worlds, and feature advanced technology such as spacecraft and video communications. The setting of this extract is a spacecraft. Meteorites and the planet Gundra are referred to. Examples of advanced technology are the visual address unit, the long-range communication system and the propulsion unit. You can use some of this evidence in your answer:

> This is a passage from a science fiction story. It is set aboard a Gundrian spaceship, with advanced technology such as a visual address unit and long-range communication systems.

Test yourself

Answer these questions about the passages.

1 Give one way in which the third passage is different from the other two.

2 What is the setting of each of the three passages?

To answer the following questions you will need to re-read passages in earlier chapters.

Chapter 1: *The Cruel Game* (page 4)
3 Which of the three passages in this chapter is Floella Benjamin's true story most similar to? Give reasons for your answer.

Chapter 3: T*he Girl at the Well* (page 10)
4 What features of an historical story does this passage have?

Chapter 6: *Grendel* (page 18)
5 What kind of story do you think this is? What makes you think so?

6 How is 'Grendel' different from the third passage in this chapter?

Answers and Guidance are given on p.34. **How long did you take?**

What's it all about?

★ In this chapter you will learn how to write down what you think about what you have read.

★ You will need to explain your opinion in quite a long, detailed answer.

★ Your National Test Reading paper will include at least one question which asks you to express your opinion.

How to write what you think

Before you can form an opinion you will need to read very carefully. You may be asked to comment on the whole or part of a passage.

Read this poem carefully.

My Mother Saw a Dancing Bear

My mother saw a dancing bear
By the schoolyard, a day in June.
The keeper stood with chain and bar
And whistle pipe, and played a tune.

And bruin lifted up its head
And lifted up its dusty feet,
And all the children laughed to see
It caper in the summer heat.

They watched as for the Queen it died.
They watched it march. They watched it halt.
They heard the keeper as he cried,
'Now, roly-poly!' 'Somersault!'

And then, my mother said, there came
The keeper with a begging-cup,
The bearer with burning coat of fur,
Shaming the laughter to a stop.

They paid a penny for the dance,
But what they saw was not the show;
Only, in bruin's aching eyes,
Far-distant forests, and the snow.

Charles Causley

Let's see if you can answer this question:

> Do you think the bear is happy to be dancing in the sunshine? (Yes/No)
> Explain your opinion, using parts of the poem to help you.

This question expects you to support your opinion by finding evidence (words and phrases) in the poem which show whether the bear is happy or not. There is one word 'caper' which perhaps suggests that the bear might be having fun dancing around, but there are many more words and phrases that suggest it is unhappy.

This is a good answer:

> I don't think the bear is happy to be dancing in the sunshine. Words and phrases which show this are "lifted up his head", "dusty feet", "aching eyes". These show the bear is tired and unhappy. The poet also uses a very strong image, "burning coat of fur", to show he is not suited to the 'summer heat'. He is used to living in "far-distant forests, and the snow".

Now let's see if you can answer this question:

> What do you think the mood of the poem is? Explain your opinion using parts of the poem to help you.

The mood of the poem is the overall atmosphere created by the poet through his or her choice of language. When you are asked to comment on mood, you need to think very carefully about the effect particular words and phrases have on you.

A good answer is:

> At first I thought it was going to be a happy poem with the children enjoying the bear's dancing, but the line "Shaming the laughter to stop" made me realise that this was really a sad poem. The last two verses are particularly moving, describing the poor bear "with burning coat of fur", now so far from the "far-distant forests, and the snow" of his home.

In poems, poets often use very striking **images** to create pictures in the mind of the people reading the poem. An image is something that isn't real but seems as though it is. Here the poet talks about the bear's 'burning coat of fur' – the fur isn't actually burning but it looks as though it is because of the heat of the sun shining on it. The poet uses this image to emphasise how cruel it is to make the bear dance in the sun when it has a thick coat suited to living in a cold climate.

You may want to do these as two separate sessions.

Session 1

1 Why do you think the poet wrote the poem about the dancing bear? Explain your opinion using parts of the poem to help you.

The following questions are about passages earlier in the book.

Chapter 3: *The Girl at the Well* (page 10)
2 Would you be interested in reading the rest of this story? (Yes/No)

Say what you liked or did not like about the story so far.

 How long did you take?

Session 2

Chapter 4: *The School Teacher* (page 12)
3 Would you like this character as your school teacher? (Yes/No)
Explain your opinion.

Chapter 7: *Eating the rainforest* (page 21)
4 Has reading this passage changed your mind about eating hamburgers? (Yes/No)
Explain your answer.

 How long did you take?

Answers and Guidance are given on p.34.

10 How writing is organised and structured

What's it all about?

★ In this chapter you will learn to answer questions on how authors organise and structure their writing.

★ Your National Test Reading paper may include questions on this.

Purpose and audience

The way writing is organised varies according to **purpose** (why it is written) and **audience** (who it is written for). The purpose of the poem 'My Mother Saw a Dancing Bear' (Chapter 9) is to make its readers understand the suffering of an animal which experiences cruelty, and to make readers sad, or even angry, about it. The poem is written for adults and children of your age or older.

A story writer organises his or her writing so that a particular audience will understand and enjoy the story. For example, an author writing a story for very young readers will use simple words and sentences, and write about things those children are interested in (for example, animals and toys that speak).

The animals played a tune.

On the other hand, a story like 'Beowulf' (Chapter 6) uses language and sentences suited to older children, and deals with a subject which would be far too frightening for younger children.

Let's see if you can answer this question:

Why has the writer of the letter in Chapter 5 (page 15) written that letter? Who does the writer expect will read it?

A good answer is:

The writer has written this letter to tell the readers of the newspaper about the council's unacceptable delay in repairing a streetlight, in the hope this will persuade the lighting department to repair the light without further delay. The writer expects the letter will be read by the readers of the local paper, perhaps including Capshaw councillors.

Structure

Each type of writing has its own **structure**. A recipe has a different structure from a story, and a letter is organised differently from a poem.

Let's see if you can answer this question:

> What features of an autobiography does the passage in Chapter 1 show (page 4)?

A good answer is:

This passage has the following features of an autobiography: it is written in the past tense and the first person, and tells about the writer's own experiences, thoughts and feelings.

Organisation

All writers, whether of fiction or non-fiction, take great care in planning their writing. Story writers, for example, organise their writing into a beginning, a middle and an ending. Each section is also organised to keep the interest of the readers. In 'Beowulf', for example (page 18), the writer builds suspense by giving readers just a few details at a time about the terrible Grendel. This makes them want to read on.

Writers of newspaper reports and articles (see Chapter 7) have to make many decisions when organising their writing:

- how to interest their readers, and how much to tell them;
- which words to use and how to use them;
- when to use short sentences and when complex ones are more suitable;
- how to help the reader by the use of headings, punctuation etc.

Let's see if you can answer this question:

> Why do you think the reporter who wrote 'The Grunt Escape' (page 20) does not immediately tell the reader that the fugitives are pigs?

A good answer is:

The pun in the headline 'The Grunt Escape' gives us a clue that the report is about pigs, but we are not told until the fourth paragraph who the fugitives are. I think the writer does not immediately say that the fugitives are pigs so that the reader will keep reading to find out who they are.

Viewpoint

Stories can be told from different points of view, but we usually see events from the viewpoint of the main character. For example, the autobiography in Chapter 1 is written from the point of view of the little girl who has just arrived in England. We see events through her eyes. The story would be different if it were told from the viewpoint of the children who were cruel to her, because then events would be seen through their eyes.

Let's see if you can answer this question:

> Who is telling the story in 'The Girl at the Well' (page 10)?
> How can you tell?

A good answer is:

The story is being told by the main character, a Roman soldier. We can tell this because it is written in the first person: 'I was posted up there as Eagle Bearer to the Ninth Legion.'

Test yourself

To answer these questions you will need to re-read passages.

Session 1

1 Why do you think the writer of 'Finding Treasure' in Chapter 2 (page 7) begins by asking the reader a question?

2 Who is telling the story in 'The School Teacher' in Chapter 4 (page 12)? How can you tell?

3 In what ways is the fictional story in Chapter 4 (page 12) similar to the autobiography in Chapter 1?

 How long did you take?

Session 2

4 How does the writer of the letter in Chapter 5 (page 15) try to persuade readers that he or she is right?

5 What is the purpose and audience of the football match report in Chapter 5 (page 16)?

6 Describe how rhyme is used in verse 3 of 'My Mother Saw a Dancing Bear' (page 25) differently from the rest of the poem.

 How long did you take?

Answers and Guidance are given on p.35.

Answers and Guidance

Here is a chance for you to check your answers to the questions. Examples are given of possible ways of answering the questions and you should compare your answers.

1 Reading information texts for clues

1 I think she did not understand the children because they were using words she had never heard before.

The words in the passage 'they might as well have been talking in a foreign language' show that the children were speaking English, but were using words the girl had never heard before and did not understand.

2 She felt confused because she could not understand why they were being so cruel.

We can tell the girl is confused because in the passage she asks herself the questions 'What was "my kind" and why shouldn't I be in the country I was brought up to love?' She cannot understand why the boys were so cruel.

3 I think she did not tell her teacher because she had learned to be tough, and thought Marmie was the best person to tell.

The girl says, 'I had learnt how to be tough during the time Marmie had left us in Trinidad.' She waited until she got home to ask Marmie what the words meant.

4 I think Marmie is her mother, and the writer uses the word 'all' to mean the rest of the family.

'Marmie' sounds very much like 'mummy'. It is likely she would explain to all the family because it was important they understood that some people were going to be cruel to them, and that they needed to be strong.

5 I think the writer means that some people would judge her by her colour, without getting to know her as a person.

Marmie explained that 'because of the colour of our skin some people were going to be cruel and nasty to us'.

 Target time for all questions: 15 minutes

 Your time for all questions

2 Using evidence from information texts

1 a Yes, because it is both ancient and made of silver.

b No, because if the owner is known it cannot be Treasure Trove.

c No, because although it is ancient it has to be made of silver or gold to be Treasure Trove in England.

d Yes, because to be Treasure Trove in Scotland it needs only to be ancient.

The evidence for all these answers is in the second paragraph, where it explains in detail what Treasure Trove is.

2 If the coroner decides something is Treasure Trove then it belongs to the Queen, or the Duke of Cornwall if found in Cornwall. The finder will be paid the full amount of what it is worth.

This question asks you to explain what happens. You will need to answer in your own words using the evidence which can be found in the third paragraph.

3 If it is not Treasure Trove the finder can keep it.

In the fourth paragraph it tells us: 'If, on the other hand, the Coroner decides that the treasure you have found is not Treasure Trove, then you can keep it.' Use this evidence but explain in your own words.

4 The words which tell us what the writer thinks about people who get nothing at all because they do not report what they have found straight away are 'and serve you right!'

This question asks you to quote words from the passage. The writer explains in the last sentence of the passage that if you do not report your find straight away it will be taken from you. The words 'and serve you right!' tell us what the writer thinks about such people.

 Target time for all questions: 15 minutes

 Your time for all questions

Answers and Guidance

3 Using evidence and clues from stories

1 The passage tells us that Eburacum had a forum, wine shops and temples.

The evidence is in the words: 'had become a sizeable town, with a forum where the place of business was carried on, and wine shops, and temples to half a score [10] of different gods'.

2 I think Kaeso was a seller of fighting cocks because the passage mentions new fighting cocks he had for sale.

The evidence is in the words: 'some new fighting cocks that Kaeso had for sale'.

3 I think 'out at elbows with the world' means he could find nothing to please him, because the passage says 'I was bored'.

The evidence is in the third paragraph.

4 The words which show the effect the girl had on him are 'her hair lit up that grey street like a dandelion growing on a stubble pile'.

This question asks you to quote words from the passage. Make sure you have used quotation marks. A fuller answer might also point out that the girl brought back colour that earlier had been 'drained out of the world and left only the grey behind'.

5 Three details that show the story is set in Roman Britain are: 'when I was a young man in Britain', 'Roman rule spread northward' and 'I was posted up there as Eagle Bearer to the Ninth Legion'.

This answer quotes words from the passage. Alternative features of life in Roman Britain which you might have referred to are the references in the text to a frontier station, a forum and temples.

6 I think the narrator will talk to the girl, and perhaps offer to help her, because he is attracted to her.

The clue to this is in the words 'you can guess the next bit, I dare say', which suggest that what happens next is not going to surprise the reader. Any answer which fits the sense of the passage is acceptable.

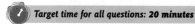
Target time for all questions: 20 minutes

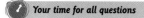
Your time for all questions

4 Understanding characters

1 The school children think he is a bit eccentric because he plays his horn and talks to himself.

The evidence for this is in the third paragraph.

2 He thinks the children are a bit cruel, but puts up with them calling him names.

The passage says the children 'can be a bit cruel from time to time', calling him names 'when they think I'm not listening, but you have to put up with that'.

3 The children do not intend to be cruel because they only call him names when they think he is not listening.

The evidence for this is 'They call me "Three Legs" or "Long John Silver" when they think I'm not listening'.

4 The words which tell his opinion of the local cheese are 'you won't find a better cheese anywhere, that's a promise'.

These words are in the fourth paragraph.

5 The villagers like living on their own in the mountains because they are used to it.

The passage says, 'We are a world of our own and we like it that way. We are used to it.'

6 Content, poor, musical

The evidence is in the words 'content with my own company and my music'. This shows the writer is content and, although living alone, not lonely. The same words tell us the writer is musical. We can tell the writer is poor from the words 'no one ever has enough money'.

Target time for all questions: 20 minutes

Your time for all questions

5 Finding the writer's opinion

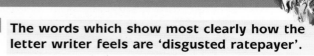

1 The words which show most clearly how the letter writer feels are 'disgusted ratepayer'.

That is the way the writer signs off the letter.

32

Answers and Guidance

2 Three phrases which show the reporter thought United played well are 'in fine style', 'tremendous determination' and 'United's tight defence proved hard to penetrate'.

Other phrases you might have used instead are 'top form', 'breathtaking save' and 'exciting goal'.

3 I think he supported United because he says 'fortunately the home side's defence remained intact through to the final whistle'.

The words 'fortunately' give away the fact that the reporter supports United.

4 The words which show Councillor Bill Evans' opinion of the improvements are 'Highstones Road will remain an accident blackspot until Capshaw Council sees sense'.

The most important words here are 'remain' and 'see sense'.

5 The reporter is not sure that the improvements will make the road safer, because he uses the words 'It may be that Highstones Road has been made safer'.

The evidence for this is in the first line of the report. The words 'it may be' suggest the writer is uncertain about the repairs. Other words the writer might have used which suggest uncertainty are 'it is believed' or 'it is thought'.

6 The word which shows the councillor's opinion of the charges is 'cruel'.

The word 'impose' shows the councillor thinks that the charges were forced on the pensioners, but it is the word 'cruel' which best shows what he thinks of them.

> ⏱ **Target time for all questions: 20 minutes**

> ⏱ **Your time for all questions**

6 The way story writers use language

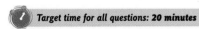

1 I think 'shrithed' means crept.

There is no single correct answer to this question. Any answer which suggests moving stealthily or in a sinister way is acceptable.

2 These words tell us that Beowulf was probably expecting Grendel, and was waiting for the right moment to attack him.

We know Beowulf recognised the Monster because 'through barred teeth he breathed one word, "Grendel".' Beowulf then waited for Grendel to approach him before leaping up.

3 'Loathsome syllables' means the horrible sounds of Grendel's name.

Loathsome means disgusting, and syllables are the individual parts of a word. Even the name of the monster fills Beowulf with disgust.

4 The author uses dots at the end of the sentence to create suspense.

This slight pause keeps the reader in suspense just a little longer. We know Beowulf is awake, but will he act too late?

5 The words which best show how powerful Grendel is are 'scooped him up' and 'ripped him apart'.

Other words which show this are 'with one ghastly claw, choked the scream in his throat' and 'within one minute he had swallowed the whole man'.

> ⏱ **Target time for all questions: 20 minutes**

> ⏱ **Your time for all questions**

7 The way authors use language in information texts

1 He reveals that the fugitives are pigs at the beginning of the fourth paragraph. The words which tell us are 'two runaway pigs were enjoying their fifth day of freedom yesterday'.

There are hints earlier in the report that the fugitives might be pigs, in expressions such as 'colour, pink with ginger bristles all over', but it is not until the fourth paragraph that the writer reveals their identity.

2 He uses these expressions because he is playing on words connected with pigs.

Reporters of light-hearted stories often use puns to amuse the reader. 'Save their bacon', 'due for the chop' and 'made a pig's ear' are all everyday expressions, here used as puns.

3 The rainforest is cleared to provide grazing land for beef cattle. By eating hamburgers people encourage farmers to clear more of the forest for grazing land. In this sense eaters of hamburgers are 'eating' the rainforest.

Although people do not literally eat the rainforest, they do eat the beef which comes from there, causing more forest to be cleared or 'eaten' up.

4 The writer uses the word 'chomp' rather than 'eat' because it means to eat noisily with enjoyment.

The words 'chomp' and 'yummy' both suggest enjoyable eating.

5 The words which first show this are 'The simple truth is, your favourite fast food snack could be doing more damage to the planet than just about anything else you come into daily contact with.'

Up until this point, the author has reminded the reader how enjoyable it is to eat hamburgers. From this point on, the writer concentrates on the harm such eating is doing to the rainforest.

6 The two words in the last paragraph which best sum up the effect of beef farming on the soils of the rainforest are 'useless' and 'wasted'.

The writer says the soil 'becomes useless for grazing. It's wasted.' An alternative answer might highlight the two words 'It's wasted'.

 Target time for all questions: 20 minutes

 Your time for all questions

8 Different types of stories

1 One way in which the third passage is different is in its everyday setting.

When comparing different types of story look at such things as setting, characters and plot.

2 The setting of the first passage is the cave of ancient dwarfs, the second is on a spaceship and the third is in a street.

Identify the setting by reading the author's description.

3 The third passage is most similar to the autobiography because it has a realistic setting and is about ordinary children.

Here it is the familiar setting and the characters which are most similar.

4 This story is set in a real place and period in history. It mentions things such as a forum, temples to ancient gods and fighting cocks which are not common today.

Look at the words the author uses in describing the setting. Which things do we seldom see now?

5 I think this story is a legend because it is about an heroic character, Beowulf, and a beast, Grendel.

These are common features of legends (e.g. St George and the Dragon).

6 'Grendel' is different from the third passage because it is in the style of a legend, having an heroic character, a beast and a mysterious setting. The third passage has an everyday setting, the characters are ordinary children, and the author writes in the style of a traditional story.

Look at such things as setting, character, plot and the words the author uses. Compare the everyday language of the passage about the runaway milk float ('I got such a fright I nearly had kittens') with that of the story of Beowulf ('the monster ripped him apart, bit into his body, drank the blood from his veins').

 Target time for all questions: 25 minutes

 Your time for all questions

9 Expressing your opinion

Session 1

1 I think the poet wrote the poem to make us realise what a terrible thing it is to be cruel to animals. The bear in the poem has been taken away from 'far-distant forests, and the snow' and made to 'caper in the summer heat'. The poet wants the reader to feel the pain of the bear, its 'burning coat of fur' and the memories of home in its 'aching eyes'. I feel sad and angry at such cruel treatment, and I am sure that is what the poet wanted me to feel.

Your answer should be along these lines. If it uses some of the same ideas and quotes some of the same words and phrases, then it would certainly be awarded full marks in the Test.

The sample 'yes' and 'no' answers to the remaining questions may be different from the ones you wrote. There are as many possible right answers to these questions as there are different opinions. A good answer will state your opinion clearly and explain why you think so, based on evidence in the text. Note that it is usually

Answers and Guidance

easier to say why you liked a text. If you did not like it, do not say you found it boring or uninteresting. Look for reasons why it failed to interest you. Good answers show that you can appreciate a passage, even though you may not have enjoyed it.

2 *(Yes)* **The writer's description of a British town at the time of the Romans is very detailed. I enjoyed imagining the streets, shops and temples of Eburacum as the soldier walked around it. I particularly liked the description of how the girl's hair 'lit up that grey street like a dandelion growing on a stubble pile'. I would like to read what happens when he stops and talks to her, as I feel certain he will.**

(No) **I liked the beginning of the story, because I thought it might be mainly about the life of Roman soldiers, and I enjoy reading about sword fights and battles. But the bright and colourful description of the girl's hair and the effect it has on the soldier make me think the story will be about them, rather than fighting. He is obviously strongly attracted to her, and as the writer says, "You can guess the next bit, I dare say", so I don't think the story will offer much in the way of sword fights.**

Target time: 15 minutes Your time

Session 2

3 *(Yes)* **I would like him as my teacher because he is kind and helpful to the children in the story. As the passage says, he is "a kind of uncle to them even after they have left school". He is patient and forgiving, because he turns a deaf ear to some of the cruel nicknames his pupils call him. I would like to hear him play his hunting horn echoing high in the mountains.**

(No) **I would not like him as my teacher, because although he seems kind and patient, he is rather odd. He spends a lot of time on his own, and talks to himself. I'd prefer a teacher who organises clubs or sports after school rather than going off alone to play a hunting horn in the mountains.**

4 *(Yes)* **I love eating hamburgers, but it never occurred to me before that this might harm the environment. I shall probably still eat hamburgers, but I will try to find out where the beef comes from, and not eat any that comes from the rainforests.**

(No) **I never eat meat, so this passage will not change that, but I never realised that those people who do eat hamburgers are helping to**

damage the planet. I would now like to find out if eating meat is bad in other ways too.

Target time: 15 minutes  Your time

10 How writing is organised and structured

1 **The writer begins by asking an interesting question to make the reader want to read on to find the answer.**

Most people would love to find some buried treasure, but how many would know what to do with it? The question is sure to make most people want to read on.

2 **The story is being told by the schoolmaster.**

The evidence for this is in the words 'so I became a teacher instead' and 'For nearly forty years now, I have been the schoolmaster here.'

3 **The two passages are similar because they are both written in the first person, they tell of past events in the narrator's life, and both describe their thoughts and feelings.**

An autobiography usually reads like a fiction story, the main difference being that the events are true.

Target time: 15 minutes Your time

4 **The writer of the letter tries to persuade the reader that he is right by suggesting that all ratepayers will agree with him.**

The writer does not know that all ratepayers will agree with him, but by saying so he hopes to persuade those in doubt that if so many ratepayers agree with him he can't be wrong.

5 **Its purpose is to report the highlights of the football match. The audience for the report is the readers of the local paper, and in particular the supporters of Capshaw United.**

The final sentence refers to United as 'the home side', evidence that this is the local team.

6 **In most verses the second and fourth lines of each verse rhyme, but in verse three the first and third lines rhyme too.**

The rhyming pattern of most verses is ABCB, where the second and fourth lines rhyme, but the pattern for verse three is ABAB.

Target time: 15 minutes  Your time

Read all of the following passages carefully and then answer the
questions that follow (pages 41–43).

Beaver Towers

Philip came down with a bump. He let go of the kite and it flew
just a little way to a narrow gap between two rocks. It settled
between the rocks and the long dragon tail curled itself round and
round in a neat pile by its side.

The little cloud that had led them safely all through the long
journey now sat bouncing on one of the rocks. As it bounced, it
changed from black to white and grew thinner and thinner. With a
faint sigh, it disappeared, leaving only a damp mark on the rock.

Philip suddenly felt very lonely. The cloud had gone, the kite
was very still as if it was deeply asleep, and the robin was nowhere
to be seen. He stood up and looked around. He was in a clearing in
the forest. Which way should he go? He didn't want to end up lost.
There might be wild animals. He had come so far across the sea
that he might be in a land where lions or tigers lived. On the other
hand, he couldn't just stay here. He made up his mind to be brave
and started walking towards the trees.

Just where the path went into the forest, the robin flew down
from the top of a bush and landed on Philip's shoulder. The robin's
happy song helped to make the forest seem a little less gloomy. Even
so, Philip shivered a little. The crooked branches creaked and the
shiny, wet roots of the trees reminded him of the octopus he had
seen in the sea. The forest echoed with the strange tick-tock music
of water drops as they tumbled down from the dark leaves on to the
trembling ferns.

The path grew narrower and brambles tried to pull him back.
As the forest became darker, the robin stopped singing. He pressed
himself against the side of Philip's neck and Philip could feel the
little heart beating fast.

They came to a rushing stream with stepping stones across it.
Philip had just jumped from the last stone on to the path at the
other side when he felt a rumbling in the ground. The robin

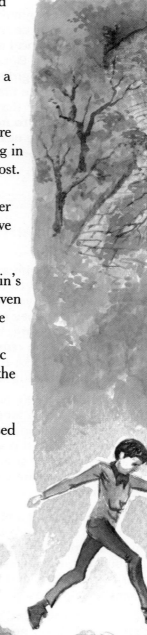

squeaked and flew into the bushes. The air grew colder and there was the thunder of galloping hooves.

Without knowing why, Philip dived into the ferns and lay hidden under some bushes as the noise grew louder. The ground shook and pounded and big chunks of earth flew through the leaves and branches. He pressed his face to the damp soil and held his breath. The noise stopped. Whoever, or whatever, it was, had halted on the path next to where he was hiding. There was absolute silence for a moment, then a growling sound.

Philip twisted his head and looked up through the ferns. Two huge black horses towered above him. The riders were dressed in red robes. They had their backs to him but he knew from the horrible noises they made that they were not men. They were sniffing the air like dogs and then growling to each other. They turned and Philip saw green eyes, black hairy faces, wolf-like snouts and pointed yellow teeth. They sniffed and started to look down towards him as if they had caught his scent.

He heard a flutter of wings and he saw a blur of red fly past him towards the riders. It was the robin. The bird darted and dived just out of reach of the snapping jaws, then landed on the head of one of the horses. Philip's chest grew tight as the rider raised a hairy claw and brought it crashing down towards the robin. At the last second, the little bird flew off and the claw hit the horse's neck. The poor beast snorted and reared into the horse in front. The two riders tumbled backwards but managed to hang onto their horses as they charged towards the stream. The horses leaped the water and Philip stood up to watch as they thundered away down the path with their riders' red robes flying in the wind.

As soon as they were out of sight, Philip ran in the opposite direction. He tripped and stumbled over broken branches on the path and his feet sometimes slid into the huge hoof-prints that the horses had left. He kept running until he could run no further. He sat down on some moss at the side of the path and listened. There was no thunder of hooves, only the drip-dropping of the water from the trees.

Making a Tree Survey

Make a survey of the trees that grow around you. Choose a garden, street or park where you think there will be a variety of trees, but start with a small area first. It is easier and more fun to do this with a friend.

When you have decided on an area, make a rough map of it with any landmarks, such as roads or buildings. Try to work out a scale for your map. (It helps to use graph paper.) Work in a definite order so that you do not miss out any trees, and then go back to identify and measure them.

What to Take

Tape measure

Pencils

Tree field guide

String

Notebook

Identifying a Tree

Try to identify the trees using this book or a field guide. Remember that there are many clues to help you recognize them, so don't use just one clue.

Making a Map

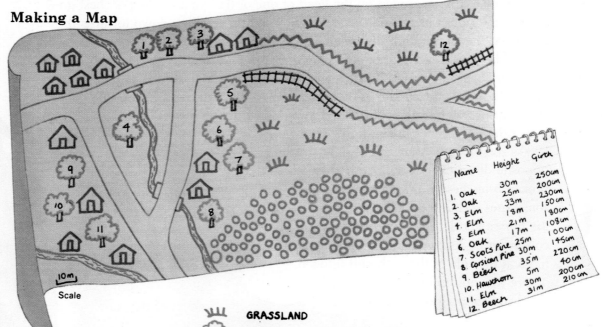

Scale

Name	Height	Girth
1. Oak	30m	250cm
2. Oak	25m	200cm
3. Elm	33m	230cm
4. Elm	18m	150cm
5. Elm	21m	180cm
6. Oak	17m	108cm
7. Scots Pine	25m	100cm
8. Corsican Pine	30m	145cm
9. Beech	35m	220cm
10. Hawthorn	5m	40cm
11. Elm	30m	200cm
12. Beech	31m	210cm

After you have identified and measured the trees (as shown above), make a neater and more detailed copy of your map. Show the scale of your map. Then make a key to the symbols you used. Here are some suggestions:

GRASSLAND

TREE

WOODLAND

STREAM

BRIDGE

HOUSE

HEDGE

FENCE

Then write down the findings of your survey. Give the name, height and girth of each tree. Repeat the survey later to see if there are any new trees, or if anything has changed.

58

Measuring a Tree

Mark stick here

Your friend is 1.5m tall.

The tree is four times the height of your friend. It is 6m tall.

Ask your friend to stand next to the tree. Hold a stick up vertically at arm's length, and move your thumb up the stick until it is in line with your friend's feet, while the tip of the stick is in line with the top of your friend's head.

Mark the stick where your thumb is. See how many times the part of the stick above the mark goes into the height of the tree (four times here). Then multiply your friend's height (1.5m here) by this number to get the height of the tree (6m).

Measure around the tree at chest height to find the girth. Ask your friend to hold one end of some string while you hold the other. Walk around the tree until you meet. Then measure the length of string.

1 Studying a Tree

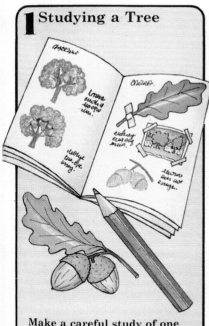

Make a careful study of one tree all through the year. Choose a tree which you can get to easily and often. Make a notebook in which you keep a record of when it comes into leaf, when it flowers and fruits, and when it drops its leaves. Include sketches or photos of the tree at these different times and specimens from it.

2

Study the animals that live in or near your tree. Look for birds' nests and squirrels' dreys in the tree top. Look on the trunk for insects and on the ground for other traces of animals, such as owl pellets, and nuts or cones which have been eaten by animals. To examine the insects in the tree top, beat a sturdy branch with a stick. Catch the insects that fall on a white sheet.

3

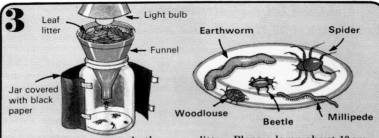

Leaf litter

Light bulb

Funnel

Jar covered with black paper

Earthworm

Spider

Woodlouse

Beetle

Millipede

Here is one way to study the animals which hide in the leaf litter on the ground. Take a large funnel (or make one out of tin foil), and place it in a jar. Cover the jar with black paper. Fill the funnel with damp leaf litter. Place a lamp about 10cm above the leaves and switch it on. Wait a few hours. The heat and light from the lamp will drive the animals into the dark jar. You can take them out and study them.

59

The Way through the Woods

They shut the road through the woods
Seventy years ago.
Weather and rain have undone it again,
And now you would never know
There was once a road through the woods
Before they planted the trees.
It is underneath the coppice and heath,
And the thin anemones.
Only the keeper sees
That, where the ring-dove broods
And the badgers roll at ease,
There was once a road through the woods.

Yet, if you enter the woods
Of a summer evening late,
When the night-air cools on the trout-ringed pools
Where the otter whistles his mate,
(They fear not men in the woods,
Because they see so few.)
You will hear the beat of a horse's feet,
And the swish of a skirt in the dew,
Steadily cantering through
The misty solitudes,
As though they perfectly knew
The old lost road through the woods...
But there is no road through the woods.

Rudyard Kipling

Reading Test questions

Here are different types of question for you to answer. The space for your answer shows you what type of writing is needed.

- **MULTIPLE CHOICE** where you need to choose the best word or group of words to fit the passage and put a ring round it.

- **SHORT ANSWERS** which are usually followed by a short line for you to write a word or phrase.

- **SEVERAL LINE ANSWERS** with a few lines for a sentence or two.

- **LONGER ANSWERS** with a box for you to write in some detail your explanation or opinion.

MARKS The number after each question tells you the maximum marks that you could gain for each question. Remember: for 3 marks you will need to write a detailed answer to the question.

You should be able to complete these questions in 45 minutes.

Beaver Towers

1   A magic spell whisked Philip away on his new kite to a far-off island. They were led on their journey by:

the stars   his friends   a cloud   animals

1 mark

2   He did not know where he was because:

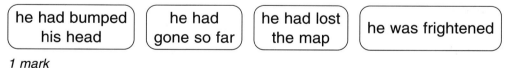

he had bumped his head   he had gone so far   he had lost the map   he was frightened

1 mark

3   Philip decided that he could not stay where he was and made up his mind that the best thing he could do was to:

find his kite   ask the robin   go back the way he came   walk towards the forest

1 mark

4   In the darkness of the trees, Philip and the robin became nervous when they heard some strange sounds. Sensing danger Philip:

ran away swiftly   hid   cried for help   prepared to defend himself

1 mark

5   What happened to the cloud that led Philip on his journey?

_____

1 mark

6   In what ways does the author tell us that Philip was nervous as he moved deeper into the forest?

_____

_____

2 marks

7   Having crossed the stream, Philip's senses immediately alerted him to the fact that he was not alone in the forest. Explain as fully as you can how this is described for the reader.

_____

_____

2 marks

8   As he hid under the bushes, Philip held his breath as the noise grew louder. Explain what happened next and what effect the author is trying to create on the reader.

_____

_____

_____

_____

3 marks

9   When Philip first caught sight of the riders, their backs were toward him but they then slowly turned to face him. What was it about these riders that gave Philip a clue as to who or what they might be?

_____

_____

_____

_____

3 marks

10 Do you think Philip is brave or a coward? Explain your answer using parts of the story to help you.

_____

_____

_____

2 marks

11 Would you be interested in reading the rest of the story? (Yes/No)

Say what you liked or did not like about the story so far.

2 marks

Making a Tree Survey

1 Before you can begin your tree study you need to do four things. Put these actions into the correct order.

A   Make a rough map of the area.   C   Make a neat copy of your map.

B   Choose a small area for your survey.   D   Identify and measure the trees.

1 ____   2 ____   3 ____   4 ____

1 mark

2 Creatures that live in leaf litter prefer to be cool and in the dark. Explain how you can prove this.

_____

_____

2 marks

3   Look at the 'Making a Map' section. The trees are numbered. Describe where elm trees 3 and 4 are situated. Use the information on the page to give as much detail as you can about each.

_____

_____

_____

_____

2 marks

4   The writer wants children to try carrying out the tree survey. Explain how the writer has organised the information to make it as clear as possible.

_____

_____

_____

_____

2 marks

The Way through the Woods

1   There was once a road through the woods. What has happened to it now?

_____

1 mark

2   The animals are peaceful and unafraid. Why do you think this is?

_____

1 mark

3   The poet appeals to our sense of hearing in several ways. Give examples of these.

_____

_____

2 marks

4 The writer uses the phrase 'misty solitudes' to describe the woods. Explain why you think the poet uses this image and what it tells you about the scene.

_____

_____

2 marks

5 The poem tells a story. Explain in your own words what the story is about.

_____

_____

_____

_____

_____

3 marks

6 The mood of the story extract is one of action and adventure. In your opinion, what is the mood of the poem? Describe it as fully as you can, referring to the poem to explain your answer.

3 marks

Answers and Guidance

National Test: Reading

Here is a chance for you to check your answers to the questions. Examples are given of possible ways of answering the questions and you should compare your answers with those given. Under each one, there is a cross-reference to the relevant skills chapter, so that you can look back at what the question is trying to assess.

Beaver Towers

1 a cloud   **3** walk towards the forest

2 he had gone so far   **4** hid

1 mark each

CROSS-CHECK   *Success in English Book 1* **CHAPTER 1**

5 **It disappeared (melted, vanished).** or

It evaporated. or

It grew thinner and thinner until only a damp mark was left.

1 mark. This question is asking you to identify correctly the clue about the cloud from the story.

CROSS-CHECK   **CHAPTER 3** Using clues and evidence from stories

6 **The robin's song made the forest seem less gloomy.**
Philip shivered a little.

1 mark for each reference; up to a total of 2.

This question is asking you to use the evidence from the story.

CROSS-CHECK   **CHAPTER 3** Using clues and evidence from stories

7 **He felt a rumbling in the ground.**
The robin flew away.
The air grew colder as if he sensed danger.
He heard the thunder of hooves.

1 mark for two of these; 2 marks for three or more.

This question asks you to use evidence from the story but this time there are several pieces of evidence and it is important that you try to use as much, or all, of the evidence in your answer. Don't just seize upon the first piece. Check whether there are other examples you can use. 'Explain as fully as you can' is a hint that there are several pieces of evidence.

CROSS-CHECK   **CHAPTER 3** Using clues and evidence from stories

8 **The noise of the hooves stopped.** or

It went quiet.

1 mark for simple answer which does not say what effect the writer wants to have on the reader.

It was very noisy and then for a moment it went quiet, making the reader wonder what would happen. or

As he lay there frightened it went quiet because the author wanted to add to the excitement.

2 marks for an answer that relates the text to the effect that the author wanted this part of the story to have on the reader.

The author builds up suspense by writing about the noise stopping and Philip wondering 'whoever or whatever it was' that was so close to him. 'Whatever' suggests something very mysterious. All the time they are making a noise he has some idea of what is going on but silence can be even more frightening.

3 marks for a full answer that explains how the author aims to build suspense, mentioning both the frightening nature of the silence and the uncertainty of what the creatures might be.

CROSS-CHECK   **CHAPTER 6** The way story writers use language
CHAPTER 10 How writing is organised and structured

9 **They looked like dogs on horseback.** or

They were ugly and frightening.

1 mark for a simple response.

The noises they made were not the noises of men. or
They sniffed the air like dogs and had wolf-like snouts. or
The riders growled and had hairy faces and noses like dogs.

2 marks for an answer that covers some of the characteristics in a general way.

They made horrible noises which were not sounds that men make. Philip could see that they 'sniffed the air like dogs' and he could hear them growling. As they turned, he could see their 'green eyes and hairy faces'. Their noses were the same shape as wolves' and their teeth were yellow and sharp. They looked and acted like dogs or wolves on horseback.

3 marks for a full answer that refers to most or all of the visual (sight) and aural (sound) clues.

This question is testing your understanding of the language the writer uses to describe the riders.

As this question is worth 3 marks you know that you have to write a detailed answer and support it with several pieces of evidence. In questions like these, it is a good idea not to quote too much direct from the passage.

CROSS-CHECK   **CHAPTER 3** Using clues and evidence from stories
CHAPTER 6 The way story writers use language

Answers and Guidance

10 **I think he was brave because even when he was frightened by the creatures he did not cry.** or

I think Philip was a coward because at the first chance he got he ran away as fast as he could.

1 mark for a simple answer that offers some reference to the text.

I think Philip was brave because it would take courage to travel by holding on to a kite. When he landed he was in a strange place but 'he made up his mind to be brave' and he set off to explore. Even when he was frightened, he still kept thinking and this probably saved him.

or

I think Philip was a coward. He tried to force himself to be brave but he couldn't help being very frightened. Instead of staying where he was to talk to the 'horsemen', he hid in the bushes. The first chance he got, he ran off as fast as he could. He was so frightened that he stumbled in panic as he ran.

2 marks for a full answer. To score the 2 marks you need to refer closely to the text and to use more than one part of the story to support your opinion about Philip.

CROSS-CHECK **CHAPTER 4** Understanding characters
CHAPTER 9 Expressing your opinion

11 **I liked the story and would enjoy reading the rest of it. I would like to know if Philip gets away and if he gets home again.** or

I didn't like the story as I do not think the robin would really sit on your shoulder like that. It's a bit silly.

These answers merit 1 mark as they do not offer a full, reasoned opinion.

I would love to read the rest of the story. I like adventures and I found the meeting with the horsemen exciting. Philip is obviously a long way from home and I'd like to read about his other adventures before he gets home, if in fact he does.

or

I did not like the story as I think it was really written for younger children. I do not think that the idea of dogs riding around on horses is going to be believed by older children and stories about animals are the sort of thing young children prefer. I prefer adventure stories set in the real world.

2 marks for an answer that gives your own opinion and supports it fully by referring to several parts of the story. A 'yes' answer and a 'no' answer are of equal value providing you explain fully why you hold this opinion.

CROSS-CHECK **CHAPTER 9** Expressing your opinion

Making a tree survey

1 **The correct order is: B A D C.**

1 mark for the correct order.

CROSS-CHECK *Success in English Book 1* **CHAPTER 1**

2 **Box 3 tells you all about it.** or
That is where they live.

1 mark for a very simple response that does not use the evidence in the text.

When you cover a jar in black paper and warm the leaf litter in a funnel, the animals will move to a darker and cooler place at the bottom of the jar.

2 marks for full answer using the evidence in the text and illustrations.

This question is asking you to use evidence from the text. The fact that there are two marks available should tell you that some detail is required.

CROSS-CHECK **CHAPTER 2** Using evidence from information texts

3 **Elm tree 3 is beside a couple of houses by the road and is 33 m high. Elm tree 4 is in a field beside the stream and is only 18 m high.**

1 mark for a simple description and a few basic details.

Elm tree 3 is with two other trees beside two houses that are at the junction of two roads. It is the biggest elm tree on the map and is 33 m high with a girth of 230 cm. Elm tree 3 is the second tallest tree on the map with only a beech tree being 2 m taller. Elm tree 4 is on its own beside the stream in a field surrounded by roads. It is nearly half the size of elm tree 3 as it is only 18 m high and has a girth of 150 cm.

2 marks for a very detailed answer that takes as much information as possible off the map and the notebook.

CROSS-CHECK **CHAPTER 2** Using evidence from information texts

4 **The writer has used writing and pictures.**

1 mark for a simple answer.

The instructions are written in steps for you to follow and there are examples of how to set up the investigations.

2 marks for an answer that gives more detail.

CROSS-CHECK **CHAPTER 10** How writing is organised and structured

Answers and Guidance

The Way through the Woods

1 It was overgrown by trees and plants. or

The weather had affected it and trees had grown over it.

1 mark

This question is asking you to look for evidence.

CROSS-CHECK **CHAPTER 3** Using clues and evidence from stories

2 The animals never saw man. or

They were not afraid because they saw so few people who might frighten or harm them.

1 mark for a simple response to the text.

This question is asking you to look for evidence in the poem and then use it to give a simple explanation.

CROSS-CHECK **CHAPTER 3** Using clues and evidence from stories

3 The poet is asking us to use our sense of hearing when he describes 'the sound of the otter whistling for its mate', 'the beat of the horse's feet' and 'the swish of the skirt'.

1 mark for two of these references; 2 marks for all three.

This question is expecting you to find several examples of the poet's use of language in the poem. It tells you in the wording of the question that the poet appeals to our sense of hearing **in several ways** so you need to look for as many as you can.

CROSS-CHECK **CHAPTER 6** The way story writers use language

4 It is all still and quiet. or

The woods are deserted except for the animals.

1 mark for a simple explanation with little reference to the poem.

The woods are deserted except for the animals that live there. As the sun goes down in the evening 'the night air cools' to form mist. It is still and peaceful with only the ghostly rider disturbing the air. The writer uses the words 'misty solitude' because these two words together describe both the quietness of the scene and the evening air.

2 marks for a full answer.

This question draws your attention to one small part of the poem and then asks you to explain an image (a picture that the poet has conjured up by his choice of words).

CROSS-CHECK **CHAPTER 9** Expressing your opinion

5 There was once a road through the wood but it has been overgrown. Nobody goes there but you can hear the sound of a horse sometimes.

1 mark for a simple outline of the story.

Once there was a road through the woods but it is now hidden by trees. Nobody goes to the woods and the animals live in peace. In the summer you can hear the sound of horse's hooves amongst the trees.

2 marks for a fuller answer that does not link the sound of the horses to the idea of a ghost.

A long time ago there was a road through the woods but it is now overgrown with trees and plants. As nobody goes there the animals and creatures are not disturbed and are no longer frightened of man. Late in the evening in summer it is possible to hear the sound of horse's hooves as if a ghost from the past is still using the old road.

3 marks for a full answer.

There are three essential elements to the poem: a) the woods then and now; b) the animals who are unafraid; c) the rider who is probably a ghost. It may help you to mark your answer to this question by awarding one mark for each element.

CROSS-CHECK **CHAPTER 3** Using clues and evidence from stories

6 I think this poem is written in a gentle mood with nobody being frightened or hurt. or

It is a quiet poem about the woods.

1 mark for a simple explanation of the mood of the poem.

I think this poem has a peaceful mood because the poet describes the creatures relaxing without the fear of man. It makes you feel calm except that you are unsure of what the horse rider could be.

2 marks for an opinion on the mood which makes more detailed reference to the poem.

I think the mood of the poem is mainly one of quietness and gentleness with the creatures living without fear of man. However, I think the mysterious sound of horses on the old road late on a summer's evening make it spooky like a ghost story. The poet describes the woods as a restful place but hints at things that cannot easily be explained.

3 marks for a full answer that refers to the poem fully.

This question is asking for your own opinion about the mood of the poem. You have to support it by using your understanding of the poem and evidence from it.

CROSS-CHECK **CHAPTER 9** Expressing your opinion